People in My Community/La gente de mi comunidad

Firefighter/
El bombero

Jacqueline Laks Gorman
photographs by/fotografías de Gregg Andersen

Reading consultant/Consultora de lectura: Susan Nations, M.Ed., author/literacy coach/consultant

WEEKLY WR READER®
EARLY LEARNING LIBRARY

Please visit our web site at: www.earlyliteracy.cc
For a free color catalog describing Weekly Reader® Early Learning Library's
list of high-quality books, call 1-877-445-5824 (USA) or 1-800-387-3178 (Canada).
Weekly Reader® Early Learning Library's fax: (414) 336-0164.

Library of Congress Cataloging-in-Publication Data

Gorman, Jacqueline Laks, 1955-
    [Firefighter. Spanish & English]
    Firefighter = El bombero / by Jacqueline Laks Gorman.
        p. cm. — (People in my community = La gente de mi comunidad)
    Summary: Photographs and simple text in English and Spanish depict
the activities of a firefighter.
    Includes bibliographical references and index.
    ISBN 0-8368-3309-0 (lib. bdg.)
    ISBN 0-8368-3343-0 (softcover)
    1. Fire extinction—Juvenile literature.   2. Fire fighters—Juvenile literature.
[1. Fire fighters.   2. Fire extinction.   3. Occupations.   4. Spanish language
materials—Bilingual.]   I. Title: Bombero.   II. Title.
TH9148.G6718   2002
628.9'25—dc21   2002066377

This edition first published in 2002 by
Weekly Reader® Early Learning Library
330 West Olive Street, Suite 100
Milwaukee, WI 53212 USA

Art direction and page layout: Tammy Gruenewald
Photographer: Gregg Andersen
Editorial assistant: Diane Laska-Swanke
Production: Susan Ashley
Translators: Tatiana Acosta and Guillermo Gutiérrez

Printed in the United States of America

2 3 4 5 6 7 8 9 08 07 06 05 04

Note to Educators and Parents

Reading is such an exciting adventure for young children! They are beginning to integrate their oral language skills with written language. To encourage children along the path to early literacy, books must be colorful, engaging, and interesting; they should invite the young reader to explore both the print and the pictures.

People in My Community is a new series designed to help children read about the world around them. In each book young readers will learn interesting facts about some familiar community helpers.

Each book is specially designed to support the young reader in the reading process. The familiar topics are appealing to young children and invite them to read — and re-read — again and again. The full-color photographs and enhanced text further support the student during the reading process.

In addition to serving as wonderful picture books in schools, libraries, homes, and other places where children learn to love reading, these books are specifically intended to be read within an instructional guided reading group. This small group setting allows beginning readers to work with a fluent adult model as they make meaning from the text. After children develop fluency with the text and content, the book can be read independently. Children and adults alike will find these books supportive, engaging, and fun!

Una nota a los educadores y a los padres

¡La lectura es una emocionante aventura para los niños! En esta etapa están comenzando a integrar su manejo del lenguaje oral con el lenguaje escrito. Para fomentar la lectura desde una temprana edad, los libros deben ser vistosos, atractivos e interesantes; deben invitar al joven lector a explorar tanto el texto como las ilustraciones.

La gente de mi comunidad es una nueva serie pensada para ayudar a los niños a conocer el mundo que los rodea. En cada libro, los jóvenes lectores conocerán datos interesantes sobre el trabajo de distintas personas de la comunidad.

Cada libro ha sido especialmente diseñado para facilitar el proceso de lectura. La familiaridad con los temas tratados atrae la atención de los niños y los invita a leer — y releer — una y otra vez. Las fotografías a todo color y el tipo de letra facilitan aún más al estudiante el proceso de lectura.

Además de servir como fantásticos libros ilustrados en la escuela, la biblioteca, el hogar y otros lugares donde los niños aprenden a amar la lectura, estos libros han sido concebidos específicamente para ser leídos en grupos de instrucción guiada. Este contexto de grupos pequeños permite que los niños que se inician en la lectura trabajen con un adulto cuya fluidez les sirve de modelo para comprender el texto. Una vez que se han familiarizado con el texto y el contenido, los niños pueden leer los libros por su cuenta. ¡Tanto niños como adultos encontrarán que estos libros son útiles, entretenidos y divertidos!

— Susan Nations, M.Ed., author, literacy coach,
and consultant in literacy development

The firefighter has an important job. The firefighter helps people.

— — — — — — —

El trabajo del bombero es muy importante. El bombero ayuda a la gente.

Firefighters help people
by protecting them
from fires. They also
put out fires.

- - - - - - -

Los bomberos ayudan a
la gente protegiéndola
en caso de incendio.
También apagan los
incendios.

Firefighters wear special helmets, coats, and boots. They wear face masks and **air tanks**, too.

- - - - - - - -

Los bomberos llevan cascos, trajes y botas especiales. También llevan máscaras y **tanques de aire**.

air tank/
tanque de aire

Firefighters use special tools, like hoses, **bars**, and **axes**. They use ropes and long poles, too.

— — — — — — — —

Los bomberos usan herramientas especiales, como mangueras, **barras** y **hachas**. También usan cuerdas y largos palos.

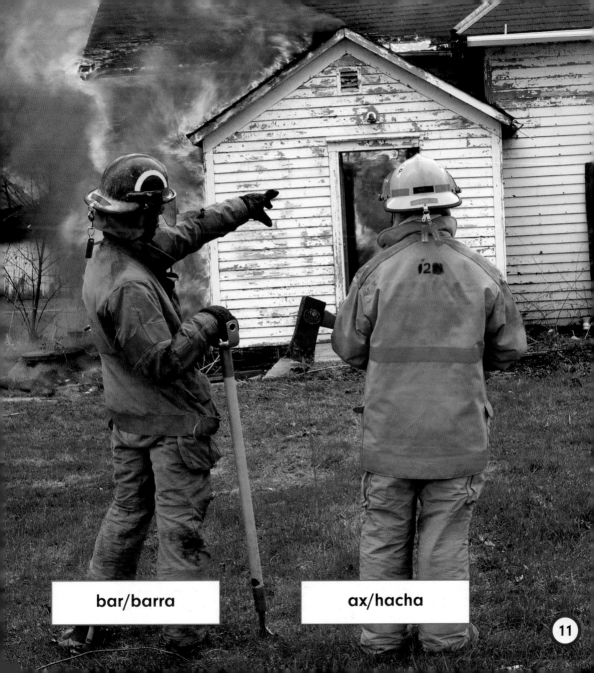

bar/barra

ax/hacha

11

Firefighters ride in fire trucks. They turn on the siren and drive very fast to get to the fire.

— — — — — — —

Los bomberos van en un camión. Para llegar a un incendio, hacen sonar la sirena y manejan muy deprisa.

When firefighters get to a fire, they use water and foam to put out the fire.

- - - - - - -

Cuando los bomberos llegan a un incendio, usan agua y espuma para apagarlo.

Firefighters use **ladders**, too. They rescue people. They give first aid to people who are hurt.

- - - - - - -

Los bomberos también usan **escaleras**. Rescatan a la gente y prestan los primeros auxilios a los heridos.

ladder/escalera

17

Firefighters visit schools.
They tell you how to
prevent fires and what
to do if there is a fire.

▬ ▬ ▬ ▬ ▬ ▬ ▬

Los bomberos visitan
las escuelas. Te
explican cómo prevenir
los incendios y qué
hacer en un incendio.

FIRE
WE

19

It looks like fun to be a firefighter. Would you like to be a firefighter some day?

- - - - - - - -

Ser bombero parece divertido. ¿Te gustaría ser bombero algún día?

Glossary/Glosario

air tanks — special containers that carry air so someone can breathe

tanques de aire — contenedores especiales con aire para poder respirar y que se llevan en la espalda

axes — tools with sharp blades on one end

hachas — herramientas con una cuchilla afilada en un extremo

first aid — emergency care that is given as soon as possible to someone who is hurt or sick

primeros auxilios — cuidados de emergencia con que se atiende lo antes posible a una persona herida o enferma

foam — bubbles that are used to put out fires

espuma — sustancia con burbujas que se usa para apagar incendios

For More Information/Más información

Fiction Books/Libros de ficción

Bridwell, Norman. *Clifford the Firehouse Dog*. New York, Scholastic: 1992.

Brown, Marc. *Arthur's Fire Drill*. New York: Random House, 2000.

Nonfiction Books/Libros de no ficción

Klingel, Cynthia and Robert B. Noyed. *Firefighters*. Chanhassen, Minn.: Child's World, 2002.

Schaefer, Lola M. *We Need Fire Fighters*. Mankato, Minn.: Pebble Books, 2000.

Web Sites/Páginas Web

U.S. Fire Administration's Kids Page

www.usfa.fema.gov/kids

For games and information on fire safety and how to become a junior fire marshall

Index/Índice

clothes, 8
ropa

fire prevention, 18
prevención de
  incendios

fire trucks, 12
camiones de
  bomberos

fires, 6, 12, 14, 18
incendios

ladders, 16, 17
escaleras

putting out fires,
  6, 14
apagar incendios

rescuing people, 16
rescate de
  personas

siren, 12
sirena

tools, 10
herramientas

visits from
  firefighters, 18
visitas de los
  bomberos

work of firefighters,
  4, 6, 14, 16, 18
trabajo de los
  bomberos

About the Author/Información sobre la autora

Jacqueline Laks Gorman is a writer and editor. She grew up in New York City and began her career working on encyclopedias and other reference books. Since then, she has worked on many different kinds of books. She lives with her husband and children, Colin and Caitlin, in DeKalb, Illinois.

Jacqueline Laks Gorman es escritora y editora. Creció en Nueva York, y se inició en su profesión editando enciclopedias y otros libros de consulta. Desde entonces ha trabajado en muchos tipos de libros. Vive con su esposo y sus hijos, Colin y Caitlin, en DeKalb, Illinois.